Common Sense

Paula Sole

abbott press®

A DIVISION OF WRITER'S DIGEST

Common Sense
Paula Sole

ISBN: 978-1-4582-0028-0 (sc)
ISBN: 978-1-4582-0029-7 (e)
Library of Congress Control Number: 2011912823

Abbott Press books may be ordered through booksellers or by contacting:

Abbott Press
1663 Liberty Drive
Bloomington, IN 47403
www.abbottpress.com
Phone: 1-866-697-5310

Printed in the United States of America

Abbott Press rev. date: 8/2/2011

The itsy bitsy, teeny tiny book of "Common Sense"

Paula's guide to:

Discovering the "Fountain of Youth;" The facts of staying thin, keeping your cholesterol low, a healthy blood pressure, retaining strong bones and looking younger all by doing absolutely nothing but following my simple "lifestyle theory." You can save money and time by eliminating the high costs of the gym or diet plans that simply do not work.

Also included are tips on how to raise wonderful, respectful children. Young mothers often wonder what steps they should take on disciplining their children and what steps to take to ensure positive results. Included in this book are helpful opinions on ensuring positive results to commonly raised questions.

How to be the woman you were meant to be" - - Janet quote

Included in this book are simple steps on how to keep a clean home.. By following my theory, you can also eliminate the fall and spring clean-up. This saves you time too.

Beauty tips for younger looking skin forever. General beauty tips to feel pretty all day.

Dirty Delish Dishes—From Me To You—easy, healthy recipes to give your children all the vegetables and nutrients needed for a balanced diet. These are easy, healthy recipes with a spicy twist!

I have also included other helpful tips on life issues.

Dedication:

I dedicate this book to my children Nicholas, Christina and Joseph. They are the ones I look up to and the reason for living.

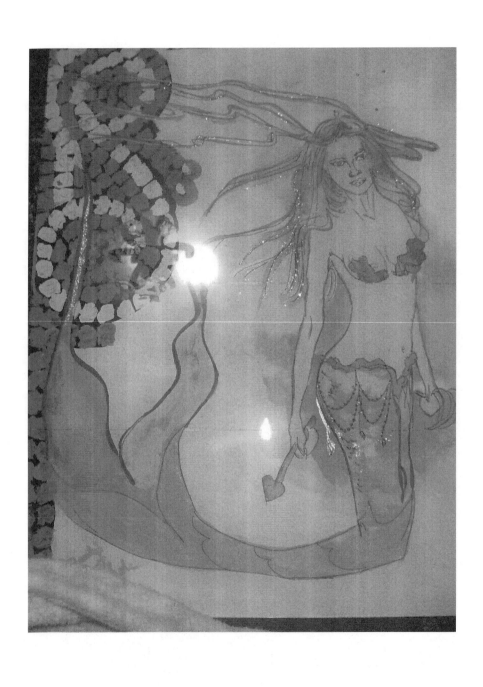

Hello, my name is Paula. I actually wrote this book at the age of 45. I am writing this book, because young people and women and mothers have always come to me for advice. I want to show people that you don't need a college degree; you don't have to listen to the "so called expert"; you do not need to join a gym; you do not need people to clog up you minds with nonsense about diets and vigorous exercise in order to live a thin and healthy life. The only thing you need to succeed in life is to love yourself truly and to have the simple common sense approach in your daily lifestyle. By following these simple steps in my book, you will say to yourself....This is so simple. Yes, it's so simple, but people do not do it because it's so simple. By following these steps, I assure you that you will be healthier following this routine. But you have to be one that has tremendous self control to start out with. Otherwise this is not for you. Once into this routine for about a month or more, your body will find it easy to do this and you get acclimated to the routine, hence a healthy way of life. So join me on a journey for you to pass down to your kids and friends on the lessons of life....The good old fashioned way.

I am a 45 year old housewife—domestic engineer, lover, artist, homemaker, chef, physician," etc.. I am writing this book because I feel I need to express myself and help others to find themselves. I am a high school graduate—Hello to the Paul Sixers"—With a partial scholarship in Art for college, I decided to go to a Court Stenography Academy to persue my education. I've come to the realization that the only way to survive in this mixed up world is to have the incredible ability of common sense! I guess I was born with it or achieved this phenomenon by my early interaction with adults at such an early age. This book will give you helpful tips on life issues. For example...How to bring up children to be strong leaders in a society; how to slow the aging process—Yes, the Fountain of Youth"; how to keep your house clean and thus, never having to do a fall or spring clean-up; how to save money; how to be happy; etc..

Let's start with just a little background of myself. Just a little....

I grew up in Brooklyn..Ah, good ole Brooklyn. It was a great experience for a child to grow up in a city. There is something to be said of " street smarts." You'll see what I mean as you continue reading. I would keep busy by walking the neighborhood and speak with all the elderly. Believe me, all the apartment houses there were filled with lonely, elderly people just sitting by their window-staring out into the streets longing for someone to talk to them or to just pass the time watching the cars and people go by. Being an artist, I have the ability to be in-tune and overly sensitive to people's needs. I have to say, it was very enjoyable to speak with these people. I learned so much from their life stories and the little tips they would give me, that I cherish them forever. Every child can learn so much from the elderly—I must say, you have to be very patient, though, to sit there for quite sometime, because they are so excited to finally have someone listening to them that they can go on and on or even repeat the same story over and over. Oh, well. Just be patient, I would say to myself. I felt so good after spending time with them that I devoted a large part of my day, each day, to giving my time to these people. Time is the best gift you could ever give someone. I felt I was being a good Christian or Samaritan. Then I would also go to stores for them and shop for them, because some could not walk well. When I would see a little old lady carrying two heavy grocery bags, I would offer to carry them for her. I would also help them cross the street. Yes, I know this sounds silly to you, but believe me....try crossing someone, holding their arms, through a six lane street. Especially one which I dreaded, but did help all the time.... There was one very poor, elderly lady who took the tiniest baby steps.... like the character in "The Carol Burnett Show" the one that walked ever so slowly.....Yes, well if you know what I mean, you are definitely laughing by now. She was so dirty and smelled so badly of urine. I felt so bad for her. But, I had to hold my breath and cross her at this intersection that was six lanes. Mind you, we are going so slow, the light would change from green to walk to red and I had to signal to the cars to please wait for us to finish crossing. All this at the age of eight. Hard to believe. Somethings, I amaze myself. Now when I reached their apartments, I would never go inside. I would leave the bag in front of their door. My parents did teach me to be kind but cautious. I guess it's also called "Street Smarts."

So what I would like to say is teach your children to speak with strangers and help others or the elderly, but always think of every angle of safety and danger. They become stronger, respectful young people by doing this. Teach them to be aware of strangers, but know their limits. Another example, do not enter a strangers' car or go too close to one when a person, for example, asks for directions. Also do not enter a stranger's home or go anywhere with them. You can be a great role model to your children by letting them watch you speak and help strangers. Show them your limits. Children pick up all the things you do. For example, when you food shop together, even your actions towards people they will pick up. If they see you talking to people and offering them to go in front of you, or help them with anything, little children pick up on these traits at an early age. If your children see you being nice to strangers, they are likely to do the same. This leads to a lasting impression, and they are likely to do the same. This definitely helps them in their future to be leaders in a society. This will give them confidence enough for them to lead when the rest or majority of children are quite the followers. Another helpful tip is whenever they arrive at someone's home or at a social event, tell them that it is a must for them to always greet everyone with a handshake or eye to eye contact. This is imperative! If they start this at an early age, it becomes second nature and they will do this all their lives. This is a very important key in self respect and respecting others. This also teaches them how to achieve their public speaking abilities. Children and people lack "people skills," and find themselves always looking for the next "self help" book or seminars on how to speak in front of an audience. By following these simple steps mentioned, children instill these good habits early on.

Let's get into eating habits. When I was a child, living around the corner from a candy store was like winning the lottery! With only 10 cents, I could buy any candy bar. Because I over-ate consistently, especially with junk food, I remember I became overweight from the age of nine through 12. By junk food, I meant all types of candy, can foods, chips, ice cream, frozen foods, etc. Believe me, my mother would cook us a lovely dinner, but anytime before, during and after, watch out or hold your plate, cause I'm comin"!! At the age of thirteen, I realized I was tired of being overweight and decided that I would do everything I can to look like a "Barbie Doll." I know that sounds silly, but when you're young and the world idolizes the beauty of Barbie, you learn that Barbie is Power!! I also couldn't understand why everyone was so thin and I was so heavy with excess weight. So, at the age of 14, I came up with my very own eating plan and lost a significant amount of weight. I became a healthy, thin young lady. I also kept up with

3

my daily routine of playing with my "guy" friends stick ball, stoop ball, run in bases, and such. Keeping active is vital and key to losing weight. Now, I had to think how can I maintain a lifestyle that will keep me thin and fit forever?!

At fifteen, I moved to New Jersey—into the country. At that time, it was the country, believe me! At the age of 16, I perfected my eating ways. So, if your goal, as a woman, in life is to have a size 0 or 2 dress at the age of 45, and do simply nothing, then follow these tips. I have to warn you, though…. This is only for those people who have strong self control and who really are serious about losing weight and keeping yourself healthy. After the initial start—about a month—this way of eating becomes very easy to do because your body wants to do it as time goes on. Nearly nothing is quite natural to the core, but this is eating as close to natural as you are going to get. You will find that your body will not crave fatty foods, sugar or processed foods. Your body stays cleansed and light/filters clean. That means your bowels will move more often. This is a good thing. It might help those who suffer from constipation. Now, if you follow this routine, you are taking it upon yourself to try a simple European lifestyle of eating. This can only help you not hurt you. Nothing can prevent cancer or certain allergies, but I bet if your body stays clean of impurities from foods, it can certainly act as an asset of preventative measures. Here are the ages and types of people to start with this lifestyle. So remember, when you bring up your children, do not stop them from eating all kinds of things. I do believe this is the time, when they are young, to eat everything. This is of the utmost importance in building very strong bones. Whole milk, and every variety of food is crucial in building strong bones. I know this because I have very "heavy" bones or lots of density of bone. This is from eating everything.

Now the age to start this healthy routine:

For young ladies 18 years of age. Remember, you can start this any time, but if you have children, you can advise them of this information.

Men 21 years of age

Hard-core Athletes will have to add the "Additional Food Consumption Part" along with the existing routine. The additional consumption will only be for the morning.

In the morning:

You can have one or two cups of tea or coffee.

Now, remember, for woman especially..... it is not true to eat your biggest meal in the morning. This only opens your stomach to crave food all day. If you keep it light, psychologically, you want to eat less.

For a food, you can have a few slices of any "all natural cheese."

You can also have any fruit or two that you want.

I will not repeat that you can have any beverage such as orange juice or coffee or tea every day.

Another day you can have a banana. Another day you can have two or three eggs. No bread or carbohydrates. This is the key. For breakfast and lunch, their will be no cereal, waffles, pancakes, cake, or breads at all.

Another day you can have oatmeal.

Another day, you can have eggs again.

Okay, that's the morning. Remember, you can eat fruit or cheese throughout the day as a source of snack.

For lunch:

A tall glass of chocolate milk---ovaltine or Nestle's Quick –is a good source of vitamins and iron.

Another day you can have tuna plain.

Another day, salad.

Remember, fruits and vegetables can be eaten too.

You can also have one cup of coffee or tea in the afternoon for pleasure. Oops....the other pleasure goes a long way too. I'm getting off track now.

The key hear is to eat anything that is light even a few slices of chicken or turkey without the bread. There will be no bread throughout the day.

Now, here is the trick....In the evening for dinner, you can have anything you like as long as it is natural and definitely no snacks!!!! Please refer to my special, healthy recipes that are located in this book. I will give you all the ideas you need for a meal. Plus, remember, they are all natural, fast and easy to make!! They will contain all the food groups so that your children grow up eating everything without complaining. It is very disheartening to see young kids only eating macaroni and cheese or chicken nuggets. If you cook them a meal and state that this is what is for dinner tonight, without giving them choices, they will learn to eat it.

Okay, when I say you can eat anything for dinner, I mean anything. Indulge yourself in everything from two plates of pasta to bread and butter to anything. Make sure you eat meats. Filet Mignon, eye round roasts are the leanest forms of beef and give you the protein you need in life. Chicken and fish are vital too. Pasta, pizza—if made with all natural cheese—is very good for you. Sometimes I make pasta and a full course meal . Eat it all!! By doing this for a while, your body is cleansed and you find that you can even eat late at night and not gain any weight.

Now, after dinner, you should only have fruit if you crave a food.

Remember, wine during dinner is very good for you. Remember, everything in moderation is good for you. Another thing, I know you only live once so the occasional all natural chocolate or ice- cream will not hurt to eat from time to time. But when you are on this meal routine, you don't feel the need for any deserts. Believe me.

Most of your meals at night should be those that are cooked from you. It is nice to go out to eat from time to time too. Just don't make it a daily routine. Some foods in restaurants have lots of preservatives or hydrogenated oils in them. Hydrogenated Oils are saturated fats and they make the food hard to break down in your body-hence the food you eat stores into fat on your body. Stay away from frozen foods, candy, snacks, cakes, and foods that contain this. I started not eating Hydrogenated oils when I was 16 years old, and I feel fabulous. When you eat light and healthy, you find that you have lots of energy and strength. Believe me, you have a lot more energy !!

If you are a cereal person, like I am, you can substitute a dinner for cereal. If I have unexpected company that arrives during dinner, and I give my portion to them….I'm very pleased to do so and I think….Yes, it's cereal tonight. So in the evening, I will eat two or three bowls of cereal and not gain weight. This is because my body is cleansed with no fat and impurities and I can afford to eat as much cereal as I want. It's so good for you. I always would tell moms how good cereal is for children.

Athletes: Follow my plan, but substitute the morning regimen with eggs w/ 2 slices bread or cereal or oatmeal. Remember, eggs are very good for you, and you can eat plenty of eggs a week. Like, for example you can have two or three eggs, three times a week.

What I am about to tell you now is the most important factor to follow along with this lifestyle is that you can not smoke any cigarettes, marijuana, consume any recreational drugs or "over do" it with alcohol. Yes, I mean it. These things really are bad for your skin and body organs. It really ages you. It makes you become dependant on them. It makes you a weak person inside and out. Now, it is important to have a social drink hear and there with dinner and friends, but when you over-do it, it just is not good for you. Now, the occasional cigar is good for you. It shows that you are worldly, and that you have self control if you can have it every once in a while. Not cigarettes, though. If you are a parent, remember, you are a parent first and a friend second. Set examples. You will be very proud to tell your children that you have never tried a drug or cigarette, and they will want to do the same. Also let them know that if they would like to smoke, that it will be "their problem." And if they want to be the best athlete, that the cigarette will hinder their ability to perform to the best of their capability. This will also teach them self control and how to be great leaders.

Allergies: I believe by following my plan that you can fight off allergies. Never take too much allergy medication, because your body has the ability to fight allergies on its own. As a child, I was allergic to everything. I might as well not be living!!! I would get shots and take medication every week, but when I started cleansing my body with my eating routine, my allergy symptoms disappeared and I never had to take allergy medicine again.

I do want to include another point…I found that people would say by eating less that you would slow down your metabolism. Well, I say to that… this is a good thing. I believe by slowing down your metabolism, you slow down the ageing process, hence, the"Fountain of Youth."Remember…you will not alter or slow down your thyroid at all. My thyroid was not affected from this. In fact, at the age of 47, my doctor could not believe that I have the body of a younger person..like a woman in her twenties. My blood pressure and cholesterol, "knock wood,"… you know what I mean… are perfect. With this theory of mine of slowing the aging process, I had to put myself through a few tests. So, I did. You will read it later in this book about my soccer and hockey escapades.

I have also read in a recent article that certain scientists, along with people in some well known university were conducting a study about a theory similar to mine. They stated that they were in the early stages and that they needed to do more studies on this matter. I tried contacting them, but to no avail, I was not successful. No surprise…if you know what I mean. I wanted to show them that my theory was living proof and that I started my theory 30 years ago. I guess they are a little too late, but they will find my theory to be truthful.

I, for one, also truly believe that a happy mind leads to a healthy body. You have to really want this for yourself. This plan or routine is not for everyone.

Okay, I'll tell you a little about the certain studies I have put myself through. During the age in which I was in my thirty's, I joined a women's soccer league and found that even with not playing one sport in my high school years or thereafter, I outlasted the younger women on the team and was much stronger. Now, remember, I am not a runner, nor do I have any soccer skills, but I had to learn and keep up with their regimen immediately. There were all kinds of women with all kinds of experiences. There were those who played in high school and college. There were younger girls who were still in college. There were those who were soccer moms who played organized sports when they were younger. There were those who went to the gym religiously." And here comes me, someone who never played and had no running experience. I know from my son how intense soccer can be. You have to be in tip top shape to keep up. Believe me, I was no great player, and the women were so kind and tough, but my point is that I kept up and was able to participate in games.

Here's a better study. In my forty's, with the encouragement of my wonderful children, I taught myself how to ice-skate. Now, you have to know this. I was very petrified of the ice and never thought I would get to ice skate. When I taught myself how to skate, that turned into speed skating, hence, ice hockey. I remember the manager of the rink came up to me and told me that I was ready for the ice hockey clinic. Without asking too many questions and excited about the whole endeavor, I found myself on a clinic with men ranging in age of 26 through 45 years of age. There were only two women, who played on a college level league who accompanied me in this clinic.

By learning very intense drills which the younger groups would do such as jumping over sticks and diving onto the ice and getting up with speed, I became pretty good right away. Being the dare-devil that I am, I found myself doing all sorts of tricks. At the age of 42, I was doing more crashing into the boards, purposely. I did jumps and tricks and I found myself having more energy, stamina, agility and speed than the younger people. I never complained and did not want to get off the ice not even for a minute. This impressed me, because osteoporosis runs in my family or you always hear doctors having concerns with osteoporosis being known to affect older women starting in their 40's or younger. From following my routine or theory, I found my bones to be strong and or with full bone density.

I tried to form a Women's Ice Hockey League for hockey moms, but found that the younger women wanted to join as well. We would get together once a week for an hour and we had women of all ages ranging from 24 through the 30's. We would have a blast! I came up with the "Paula Move!" I loved it. This move was fabulous. I would skate really fast, go down onto my knees and go into a split on the ice- - then blast a shot into the goal. This is where my cheerleading in grammar school came into play. Next, I found myself on the front page of the Star Ledger, thanks to the wonderful reporters of that newspaper. Well, this is all good fun.

So, I find that it might not be true when people state that they wish to be younger in order to have more energy. They wish for the good ole days of being younger and having more energy. Or another important point I would like to state again. Maybe osteoporosis can be altered or stopped when people follow my eating routine: the important theory of eating everything as a child to build a strong core or strong bones and then at a certain age, when it counts, to get into a more healthy eating routine. Remember, I believe that if you starve or deprive your children of fatty foods when they are little, when they grow up, they indulge to the extreme because they feel that they missed out on something. They feel they missed out on eating al these different types of foods. So do it my way. Give it a try. It can't hurt.

I want to get into another subject. As a woman, the greatest work out is-------cleaning your house!! I mean really keep your home in tip top shape. If you do this, you never need to join a gym, because you will keep active and stay in shape. You'll have a home that everyone would love to come to. Your home will stay newer longer. You also will never have to do the Spring or Fall clean up, because you have kept up with it. There are many benefits. Remember, less is better. By that I mean…do not fill your home with clutter and too much furniture. A light and airy approach works best. Never waste your money on unnecessary items. Purchase items with value. Furniture of value and classic styles will be in your home forever and can be passed down to your children. You save money, because there is no need to change your furniture often. Keep your home painted in light colors. White is fabulous for a clean and happy look. It reflects light the best. Colors should be a hue. You should have at least two rooms with dark colors as your "statement rooms." Less wall to wall carpet is preferable. Hardwood floors are a must!! Marble and tile are elegant too. Having more bare floors is easier to clean and maintain. Less dust accumulates too. Dust is one of the most crucial forms of allergies. That's why keeping a clean home helps your family stay healthy too. Keeping a clean home also prevents mold from forming onto your home. This is a bad source of allergy also. Tips on the prevention of mold is explained on the next few pages.

Keep your bathrooms clean enough so that you can eat off the floors". Just an expression, guys. Your house is a reflection of yourself. I found that the best cleaners that you need are very inexpensive and do the trick with ease. Dish soap. This is great in taking out stains in clothes or cleaning your floors. It is very mild too. A powdered cleanser....I don't think I'm allowed to name them.. but I think you know what two types of brands I am speaking about. This product has been around for years. This is super great on getting out scuff marks on walls or the face of the steps. It is gentle too and will not take the paint off. It only will take the paint off if you have a flat based paint. So do not use it on flat based paint. It is ideal with eggshell or high gloss brands. Well, onto something else.

Keep your kitchen as a showroom. After cooking or after each meal, unset the table and keep your counters free of clutter. Keep pretty things on the counter. Have a draw in your kitchen for mail. Have a draw for papers, pencils, pens, scissors, calendars, etc. Always put everything away immediately in its space or spot so that you will never lose anything. Keep your keys in always the same spot so that you know where to retrieve them. This works, believe me. Keep your garage clean and clear. Keep all equipment and stuff onto only one side of the garage. Mice and insects love clutter, so keep your home neat. Keep the side of the garage where you park your cars completely clear of debree. You might be saying...what? I have so much stuff." Well, that's what I meant when I said less is better. Sometimes people buy every gadget and item and they think they will need. Only buy when absolutely necessary. I have a husband and three children and have a lovely garage. This is where you save money and also bring up children who will appreciate the little things in life. For example, when my kids were younger, we only had the basics or essentials necessary for them to play with. They had a football, soccer ball, baseball and bat and a bike. Kids don't need every single toy. They will not appreciate things if they have everything. For the outside landscape of your home, keep all trees and bushes away from the home. Let air circulate. This helps keep animals, rodents, bugs and mold away from your home. Even keep your curb and street clean. This makes a big difference. I learned this from "Uncle Tony." He was a dear neighbor of mine many years ago.

Believe me, my house is the party house. I have always had parties, gatherings and social events. I love children and people. We've had things break too like furniture, basement banisters and even walls. That's life and what makes home a home. Always make your home inviting. Make people feel that your home is theirs too. After a gathering when everyone is gone, then clean up everything. Put everything in its place even if it's late. Then go to bed. I know you are tired, but this is a great workout and you will feel better in the morning.

Oh, a must in the décor area. Every home should have crystal chandeliers. This is a great way to reflect light in your home. It looks elegant and makes a great statement piece. An outstanding mirror or rug goes a long way too. The décor that I prefer is Italian Baroque, English, French Country and definitely have the great table!!! What do I mean by "The Great Table." This is the core gathering place where your family and friends will be at all times. A wonderful large, wooden Italian farmhouse table is warm and inviting and sets the tone for love, happiness, laughter and feeling at home.

As a mother and wife, the most important goals of all is your husband and children. I have been very fortunate to have a husband who worked so hard all his life just so that I can stay home with the children. Thinking back, there were some hard and difficult times. I remember so many things like how were we going to buy a Christmas tree or even gifts. I remember all three children sleeping in one room and most of the time the youngest child had to sleep on the floor in the living room because we did not have enough room. This was a tiny house, but we made it a home. We had the best parties and times there. It's all what you make of it. That home was so cute and the children felt happy there with the pretty windows capturing the light through the lace curtains that I used to make myself. My kitchen's theme was English Tea time with all the pretty, tea cups lined along the kitchen counter. Okay….I'm getting off track.

I chose to stop working and be a "stay at home" mom when my first son was born. Even though I had a scholarship for Art, I decided to Stenography school instead. I had my own agency, but I decided to stay home and raise my children. I felt that being a stay at home mom was the right thing for me to do. I wanted to give my children all the love and lessons from myself. Believe me, there were many years of never going out for dinner, no vacations, not buying any new clothes. But my husband and I always knew that our children were our first priority. So we sacrificed money and our lives for our children. We always had wonderful family and friends to gather with and have a good time with. That's the one thing we spent money on which was "FOOD!" Yes, food is the key to happiness and social gatherings. We were always grateful for our friends and family and wanted to show our appreciation to them through our food. It is very important to surround your children with people in your home. This makes everyone happy and become closer in your life. It also teaches them to mingle with one another.

Ladies or men, remember always choose a mate with strong character and one who has family values and goals. I know I have my husband to thank for my being able to stay at home, but you have to be smart enough to pick someone who thinks like you in the important moral value.

People also think you have to have two incomes to survive. One parent can stay home. One has to learn to wait for things. Children are first, and the material things come later in life. When you bring up your children in different stages, like we did, they see what it took to get there like good hard work. Then, they appreciate you and everything that you have done to get them there. They know...Children know at very young ages the character of their parents. Set goals and examples.

The traditional role as a woman to your mate.....Always know your place. You are a woman and he is a man. You are both different. Always be ready to listen, never complain, never nag. Always be ready to give him a massage after a long day at work. Always prepare his food after a long day of work. Never, ever say no to......

Always wear pretty things to bed. Lingerie is a must.

Now thank God I have a husband who worked so hard so I can stay home with the children. I have to say, it was very good for my kids to see us move up in life. They remember the struggles we went through to achieve our goals. They saw us move from a two family cape with Joey sleeping on the floor because we had no room to a moderate home and then to the "American Dream" home. We all learned to appreciate life and things in these stages.

Now, for the women who choose to work or who have no choice but to work....Us women have to learn to stick together. A woman should be proud if she chooses to be a stay at home mom or a working mom. Whatever makes you happy...that's what I say. For those women who have to work, they are great role models to their children and show strength to all. I remember always helping those moms that had to work. I would always open my home to their kids just to give the moms piece of mind for the day. We have to stick together. I remember having those kids almost every day, all day. They became part of the family.

Saving money.....

Make sure you have a conservative mind set. When you purchase furniture for your home, buy only classic, very good items that you really love so that you have them for a long time or forever. If you purchase heirloom quality, this can be passed down to your children in the future. If you can't afford good things in the beginning of marriage, either wait or purchase good things now, but with the intention that you will purchase fine quality in the future and never again.

When you purchase clothes, don't over-due it. Buy things that you really need and remember, you can wear a pant or skirt three times a week by changing your top or blouse to create different looks. No one will know the difference. Buy only shoes that you need. For the kids, they need only one pair of good stylish sneakers and one pair of shoes. This is usually done in the beginning of their school year. Only when they are worn, do you buy a new pair. Oh, if they need sport shoes, definitely buy them.

When you have children, it is important to entertain at home a lot. This makes it fun for the kids to grow up in their home with adults and kids. They watch how you do it so that they learn to love people and they remember the good times shared. This gives them opportunities to interact and speak with adults. My parents did this a lot and I learned that I loved this lifestyle and now I am doing this. I know my kids will do this when they have their families.

When your kids are very young, take them out to dinner with you. By doing this, they get used to behaving in public. You will be very proud one day. Yes, take them to upscale restaurants too. Try not to leave them home with babysitters. Try to take them everywhere. By doing this at such a young age, they learn to be with you, enjoy your company, and want to go out with you even when they are young adults. If you have to leave them home, I strongly suggest them staying with parents.

Teach your children to have self control. A little trick to this could be as simple as this. I know this sounds silly, but this sets the tone for other things....For example:

When they go to other people's homes, tell them not to ask for anything to eat or drink. Wait for the host of the home to ask or offer a drink to you first. Then maybe accept it if you really need it. But if you're at a party, of course , they can eat and drink when they are told they can start.

Another trick to self control is before you leave your house, make sure they went to the bathroom. I mean potty-trained kids. When you're out, let them get into the habit of waiting to go home or their destination to the bathroom. Public bathrooms should be a "no, no". Of course they can go in an emergency. I see parents always taking their kids from store to store to the bathroom. The kids are doing this for attention. This is how poor self esteem or poor self control habits can start.

Another very important fact ....Never bother your kids with chores for them to do. No allowances either! You are the mother, and this is your responsibility. If you consistently keep your home and kids rooms spotless and clean, your kids will grow up to be responsible adults. Yes, I did say their rooms too. Let me explain...

Don't wait for them to clean their rooms . Just do it every day routinely. Every morning, go into their rooms and make the beds, put everything away. This keeps you a close knit family. They do appreciate it too. Never, ever snoop in their drawers. Do not ever invade their privacy. Remember –Trust!! You need them to trust you too. By not bothering them to do chores, they can concentrate on their school work and sports activities. They need all the time for this and this puts no excuses not to fulfill their homework duties. By doing all the cleaning, they, in turn, want to keep the house and their room neat because they automatically get used to this kind of neat environment and like things being that way. They also will help you with whatever you want when you ask for help, because they learn to appreciate you. Believe me, I grew up with doing everything for myself and all my own chores. This way works better!!!

Believe me, you learn how to manage your time when you do a lot of things for your children. That's what it's all about. Try to get involved in anything that you can. It teaches your children how to volunteer or be involved in your community or just how to help someone. I devoted my life to volunteer work. I was everything from the town mom to being a coach, an assistant coach, VP of the Booster Club, Booster fundraising and promoting a bon-fire event, Catechist teacher, PTA, church events, hospitals, old age homes, the list goes on. There was so little time for anything, but I always made time for playing with my kids and cooking. Spend lots of time with them. Try to teach them how to catch a ball, ride a bike, drive a car... anything you can think of that is easy for you to teach. Of course driving a car is taught when they are older and after their six hours of time taught with a professional. Just the simple thing of time goes a long way. My children and I always had time to play outside and get the kids in the neighborhood to join in. This was when they were little, of course. Then, as they got older, they knew how to do this on their own. They would play in the street and have imaginary bases for baseball. They became very resourceful and clever. It reminded me of my days in Brooklyn and the street smarts that comes with growing up in a city. I was so proud of them.

When summer would arrive, my children and I never believed in camps.. We felt that the summer was "down time." We actually felt that down time leads to success. You don't want your kids to be burnt out when they get older. Some children do so much throughout their early years and are forced by their parents to do so that when they reach those college yeas, they ultimately quit everything. They get "burnt out" an expression I would say.

I remember there were times when they would say that they were bored. This was very rarely, though, because we always seemed to be doing something. So when they would say this, always remind them that boredom can be a good thing. I would say....."Remember those days when you're doing so much and you are doing so much homework?" Well, next time that happens, think to yourself how nice it would be if you were bored right now. Boredom is a time for meditation and calmness. If they learn to accept boredom, they learn to be calm in certain situations and think. It leads to satisfaction. Almost like yoga but without doing anything physical. Yoga for the mind, I would say. When kids always do things, they become too anxious and scattered. So please teach them how to appreciate boredom.

Let's change the subject a little and talk about beauty tips and women. Always take care of yourself especially after having children. This is good for yourself and your husband will admire it too. Always wear pretty skirts and feminine attire. It's nice to invest in high-heeled shoes. Never leave the house without lipstick. A little mascara and blush for the cheeks is nice too. Even if you do not work outside the home, it is very important to feel pretty and look your best. Get dressed up. This gives you self esteem too.

A lovely ritual for younger looking skin is to make sure you place a fragrant cream all over your body every time after you shower. This is a must!!! When you come out of the shower, put your favorite cream onto your moist skin from your shoulders, back and to your toes. This is when you get the best results from the cream because your pores are open and it will absorb all the moisture from the cream. For your face, I use a brand that has three words and the two words start with the letter "O." Hope you can figure that out. Believe me. I've been doing this since I was sixteen years old, and my skin is as soft as a baby's skin. This ritual also keeps your skin looking younger and smelling pretty too.

Another thing is to always have pretty things to wear to bed. This really makes you feel like a woman.

If you're not into sports, and if you follow my eating routine along with keeping busy cleaning your home and juggling a busy lifestyle, it is important to do a five minute exercise routine about three times a week, if you'd like. This is not necessary, but it is good for you. First do some stretching. Place your hands over your head and stretch from one side to the next side. Then sit down on the floor with your legs spread eagle.

Try bringing your head down slowly toward your knees. Go as far down as you can. Little by little, if you do this everyday, you will touch your head or nose to your knees by just repeating this. Then, do about twenty sit ups. Lay on your back and fold your knees. Just pick your head up to your knees. Then you can do twenty leg lifts, Lay onto your side. Bring one leg upward and then bring it back down. After you have done twenty, switch onto the other side and do the same. That's all you need. Another wonderful form of exercise is doing a fast pace walk. Just walk as quickly as you can. If you get tired, slow down your pace and keep walking. Then pick the pace up again. This walk could just be less than five minutes. That's it. You don't need much.

The key to getting to know your children and having your children want to confide in you is......"The Family Dinner ." Communication is the key source of family trust. What better time to get everyone together in a relaxing environment and enjoy food, laughter and each other. Yes, the family dinner is the most crucial time as a family unit. Cooking is a very crucial factor in making a happy home complete. No matter what activities there are in a day whether it be school related or sports, always remember to cook a dinner and sit down and eat together. Yes, it can be done. I've done it with the busiest of schedules. With three kids, being by myself and having to juggle homework, the children playing outside or inside, sports, travel sports, taking care of others, volunteer work and such, there was always that time where everyone came home and ate dinner together. If friends were over or wanted to join, let them come too. The more the merrier, I'd say!! Eating together as a family is the key element and time to mold wonderful children. This is a time to sit down and discuss situations of the day. For them to explain to you the events of what happened in school, at a friends house or at a sporting event. If they seem sad, try to help them with a solution. It gives you the opportunity, as a parent, to ask questions, tell your own stories, to explain your troubles { in general with not too much detail in the horrible events} and how you overcame those trouble-some situations, to set the tone for events that happened in your life. You can also exchange thoughts on life, current events, their philosophies on life issues, how you helped others or just to simply "talk." If you all discuss experiences and thoughts and feelings openly, you will have secure children. Always reinforce their good behavior and their self respect for oneself and their brothers or sisters, their teachers, their elders and others. Remind them of their goodness and good deeds. Embrace their words. Respect them too as intelligent , important individuals.

Additional Tools that build confidence:

A very important theory of mine, especially if you have boys, is to make sure your boys take some type of martial arts or self defense class when they reach around 13 to 15 years old. This is a good age to start, because they are old enough to understand and remember the concepts very well. As young men, this enables them to feel strong inside and out. When your boys reach puberty, at around 15, I also suggest them to work out with weights. A man who has a beautiful core physique shows people that he has confidence, self control and cares about himself. It also shows strength and respect. People will respect him if he has a neat appearance. Another reason to know self defense and working out is because when people are nice, sometimes children think they are not as strong. This gives them the power and advantage to help themselves in certain situations if issues arise.

Cursing:

Don't be paranoid of boys who curse or if they have a vulgar mouth at times. Know your limits on certain things. Teach them that it is not nice to curse in front of girls or their peers. When they are with the guys," then that is natural to curse here and there. But in the home, try to be careful.

With girls, it is very important that they speak without cursing especially in public. It never ceases to amaze me when I see young girls dressing so femininely and then they point their fingers in everyone's face with vulgar movements and a mouth of hell. They are so mixed up. They try to look like a girl and then act like a guy. Please do not do this especially on TV or in public. You do not look good. Besides....beware, it's usually the girl who acts as a lady that can womp you one good!!! "Womp"...a word I made up referring to a blow in the face with a fist. I had to throw that in there for my cousin Gina!! Inside joke.

School sports....

Sports are a very good thing for your kids to consider to join when they are in school. This keeps them busy and gives them the opportunity to find their talents. It is very good to belong to something and contribute to your school. This helps them in their future endeavors with college admission too. Most of all, it keeps them focused on positive ventures in their life.

Music is also very important. Encourage them to try a musical instrument or to sing in a choir. This is a wonderful source of exercise for the brain too.

Religion:

Carrying tradition is a very important rule for any family. Religion is the core and source of order in a society. Bring up your children to respect God or whatever religion you follow. People get all caught up in religion and its message. I tell them to take all the things you agree and like about that religion and hold onto that rule. You don't have to go to Church every Sunday. The sacrifice is good, but, all in all, God wants you to be a Good Christian and follow in his footsteps and help others. Do support your Church with volunteer and monetary donations, if you can.

Boys wearing their hats:

It is very important to teach your sons to take their hat off when they enter a classroom or if they enter a home. This is very important to do when they speak to a lady or to their peers.

Tattoos or body piercing:

Always remember that your body is your sanctuary. It is a symbol of well being and respect. As an artist, art should only be done on a canvas or walls. Remember, this is only an opinion, but a very important one, if I may. When someone puts a tattoo or piercing on their skin, it is usually a sign of insecurity or an issue that lies deep within their soul. Why advertise that insecurity. People still see that type of bodily image as a symbol of "low" standards or a deep problem that is bothering you. Show strength and do not turn to this form of rebellion. Face problems head on and divert issues into working out or running or take up some type of hobby.

Cell phones:

Cell phones should be given to kids when they turn thirteen. They should have the standard type phone. Blackberry or I phones should be for those young adults entering college.

Remember that at the dinner table or when together, your kids should not play any video games or text or speak on cell phones when you are together. Show respect for each other.

Television in the car:

When I am driving and see kids watching television in the car, it just reminds me of another money making scheme for the car companies and another way for children and parents to disconnect. It also shows that a parent has no self control with their children and they need another gadget to keep their kids occupied.

The theory of allowance and other circumstances.....

Do not give your children an allowance. Teach them that they have to do things or help you out of the goodness of their hearts. Do not give them money so easily. Make most of their lunches. Give them money for lunch only once in a blue moon." Do not buy them every gadget under the sun. Let them wait for things. You can give them the "big" gift during Christmas or birthday. Learning to wait for things they want makes them appreciate things. If they get money for their birthday, have them save some and spend some on themselves. Do not spoil your children. They will grow up resenting your decisions and they want you to set goals. Children want to hear "NO". It gives them the excuse that they need on why things are the way they are......They want to tell their peers and friends that their parents are strict. This is the way it is in this house and that's it. Tell your children that if they live in your home, they have to abide by the rules of the home.

The theory of punishment.......

When children are small, always think twice about the punishment you give. Be consistent and follow through on the punishment. If it's a light punishment, you are more likely to follow through on it. If you do not fulfill your punishment, your kids will walk all over you and know they will get away with things the next time.

Teach your children that when you go out, whether it be to the store or other, that they not ask you for things. Before you leave your home, make sure that they have gone to the bathroom, eaten, and that they have drank their water. They are not to ask for anything like juice, or toys when you are on a mission. It is up to you to tell them that you are planning to take them for lunch or dinner or if you want to take them to the store for a treat. This keeps them from carrying on in the stores like when you hear children screaming and crying for that candy or toy. Children need to hear the word "NO" in their lives with no reason after that. Just a firm No, or just tell them that you do not want them to grow up spoiled. Explain once or twice and the rest they will know why.

Bullying and School........

Always teach your children to respect their teachers. Be on guard too. With the values you teach them, they will know when to respect their elders, but be strong enough to correct their elders too. Never get involved in altercations or situations that happened with your kids' teachers or coaches. Teach them to speak themselves to their teachers or coaches. They have to solve these situations themselves. Their teachers will appreciate this too. Teach your kids to tell you their grades to you so that you don't have to look it up in their teacher files because you trust them and want them to have their privacy.

Always teach your kids to help others or those students who appear lonely. Talk to everyone. Help those who are alone. If you see a situation that you feel you can help save them, if it is not life threatening, try to help that person or go to an adult in private and get them help. Once in a blue moon, ask them, "What did they do for someone today?" You don't realize how being nice to someone can really be saving their life or just making their day.

Bringing your children to someone's home.

This is a must!!!!! Most people do not want to bring their children to someone's home because they feel they will not behave and will touch everything. Or some people do not want you to bring your ill-mannered children to their home because they are worried they will destroy their home. At a very young age, bring your children with you everywhere. Be strict and teach them that when they are in someone's home, not to touch anything. You can teach your children this by when the minute your children are born, do not remove anything of value in your home. Do not put it away. Keep everything out. When they are infants and start to walk they will want to approach and touch things. This is the time to watch them and when they go to touch that fragile item, tell them "no touch". Gentle". If they go to touch it again , repeat the no touch. You can say gentle and place their tiny finger on the item and say easy. Like this they feel it. If they go to touch things, just repeat the "no" series and distract them to do something else. If they will not listen, give them a little tap on the hand and say, "No touch." This will work, believe me. When they go to other peoples home, they will listen to those words and never touch anything.

Teaching your children to eat all kinds of food....

A special way to make your children eat everything from fish to vegetables to meat is to just say....."This is what's for dinner". Whatever I made for dinner is what we are eating. Do not serve them anything else or substitute with chicken fingers or macaroni and cheese. This really works. They get to taste the food, and they learn to like it. I have included some easy delicious recipes for you to try too. Your children learn that you sacrificed for them. They also learn to appreciate the time it took to prepare their meal. This is the good "old fashioned" way.

Trusting and respecting your kids....

Always trust and respect your children. If you do this, they will not want to let you down. Give them lots of love and hugs and kisses. Tell them you love them. Give them their privacy too. Never snoop in their draws or computer files. This is a must!!! When you clean their rooms, just put things away and leave the room. If you do this, you show them you trust them. This is the greatest gift for them and yourself. They will tell you things that you should know. If you bring them up with the simple steps displayed in this book, they will not do anything wrong that you need to know of. Listen to them. Laugh with them. Be a parent first and a friend second. This is very important advice. It is okay for you to say No" to things. Sometimes children want the excuse of telling friends that they can't do things because they will get "In trouble" with their parents. This sets boundaries that they want and need. It gives them a conscience. Very important. "A Conscience." I learned that quote from my son, Nicky. I remember once my son Nicky told me that "rules and religion make a person have a conscience. A conscience makes a person think twice before making decisions. Religion makes a person think about Heaven and Hell; hence which decision to set forth. Wow....I couldn't believe it. I was proud and learned from him now.

Getting kids to do their homework…

If you follow my theory on doing their chores for them and not bothering them to help you every minute of the day, this will give them encouragement to do their tasks that are important for their life. In other words, they feel the obligation to do their homework because they have the time to do this. They appreciate you doing things for them so they feel this is what they have to do for themselves and for you. This is their most important obligation for the day. Doing their homework.

If you tell your kids to do their homework as soon as they come home from school, this will give them more free time to play the rest of the day. Tell them their mind will be free and clear and they will be able to have more fun knowing that their work is already done for the day. If they start this young when they are in grammar school, they will just automatically do it when they come home. You'll see them come in, greet you, grab a snack and start with their homework. How cute!!

Video games….

I always tell parents to let their children play video games. Video Games are a very good tool and exercise for the brain. It keeps the brain able to function in today's economic time. This is a very good source for teaching the brain to multi-task and to "think outside of the box."

If you follow my preliminary steps from the beginning of my book on letting them play outside, completing their homework when they come home from school and such, they only spend a little, sufficient amount of time on video games. You do want your kids to keep up with the times.

So all in all, my most crucial opinion I can give any woman is to be a "Stay at Home Mom." Now, calm down. I know there will be lots of women saying …No way". But remember, this is only my opinion, and it is great advice though. Believe me. I've been given a gift to see things for what they are or what they appear to be. I have been able to predict things that have happened. Maybe this is a gift from above or just something taught to me from my experiences in life or just an intellect of Common Sense that exists in my mentality. You do not have to take this advice, but just think about it. If you look at most young ladies today, even though they were brought up to be totally independent and have been taught that they have to be as strong as men, they are the most confused and they have the most insecurities of self worth.. Young ladies today are confused of their role. They are expected to be everything. Then, they wind up not accomplishing the most important task of all and that is just being a "lady." { examples: do not give yourself to men for selfish reasons; do not have a vulgar mouth in public; do not carry yourself as a man in wanting to fight in public.} Then they get burnt out, because they feel they must go in every direction and wind up failing in their marriage or child rearing.. I see that they are confused and do not know why they are making poor decisions in their relationships. This has to do with the pressure placed on women in our society of being "Wonder Woman." When you give mixed messages to a young girl that she has to be soft, beautiful, strong, skinny, independent, as professional as a man, a model, a super athlete, as sexual as a man, a goddess, a mother, etc., they don't know their real role as a woman and start to do everything with confusion and for everyone else but themselves. What is wrong with being just right? What is wrong with not going to college. College is not for everyone. There are plenty of intelligent young people who do not attend college. They may be even more intellectually stable than those who have attended a college. I say to those businesses out there to give young, aggressive children a chance in their field of business. This is because if you live with good, strong roles as a man or woman, the goals are set and very clear in achieving stability in life. This will make life much easier and the future will have stronger children being raised in a society. Children need a parent at home- - Not a nanny, not a cook or house cleaner. They need a mommy. They need to know that mommy is there for them, to listen to them when they get home from school especially if something bad happened that day. They need to release their fears or unhappiness the minute they walk in the door. They need mommy, because mommy cares about them and will do everything she can to make things better. Men need to appreciate a real woman. A woman who puts her man and children first and herself last, is a very powerful woman! Yes, when you put everyone first, they appreciate you and want to help you and put you first. The instincts and roles of a man and woman are etched in our biological chromosomic being. {made up word}theoretically sound. You can't change the inevitable. That's why there is so much chaos and confusion in our young men and women today. Just make it simple, if you can. This will lead to a better, happier life. When you bring children into this world, it is your responsibility to bring them up.

The truth to success is to love yourself. By following these steps, you will learn to love yourself because you know that you have done everything possible to keep a happy and healthy family and home. With truly loving yourself is to truly find happiness. If you have purchased this book, please abide by these simple guidelines:

If you are a working mother or father, you will find by maintaining my eating plan, you will have lots of energy all day.

By maintaining a clean home or apartment, you will find you have more time to spend with family, friends, or just relaxing for yourself.

The key to happiness and well being is surrounding yourself in a positive environment.

Another key aspect is to make sure you connect and meet your neighbors; keep in close contact with friends and family.

Remember, truly love yourself for you will find happiness and others will follow.

My children are young adults now. I am very proud of them. They are strong leaders in their community, but they are very kind as well. They have wonderful friends too.

I have to say…..I find myself learning from them now. They teach me to be strong, grounded and to forgive. I thank God everyday for my three children. At times I wonder….What did I ever do to deserve such wonderful kids.

I have to add that all this would not be possible if it weren't for my husband, Nick. He dedicated his life to working hard to build his business. With all our struggles, he never complained and worked diligently just so I can stay home with the children so that they can have their mother there for them. That is a selfless and true hero. He has made the strong foundation for the home. I guess he is the anchor{strength for the end result } that keeps the ship {the kids and I in the home } grounded .

I have to say a special thanks to my parents for their good advice and great moral values taught to me in the home. Yes, we do differ in life issues and opinions at times, but I tell my kids this. I took all the great things I admired about my parents and implemented those things in my lifestyle. In other words, you take the good things and do those the same, but the things you didn't agree with, you do better.. They will do the same when they grow up. They will do the good things that they like that we did and they will also do the other things better. That's what a homemaker is all about. Parents are learning as they go too. The best advice is to do the best that you can be as a parent, because there is no going back, no second chances. Be a positive roll model, and they will admire that.

I have to also thank my mother for being there for me when I came home from school. I also would like to thank my mother and mother in law for their great advice on cooking recipes and tips. This is vital and crucial for the core family gathering. Food is one of the passions in life, and it feeds the soul. Thanks to my father for all his stories and making us laugh at those family gatherings. Every home needs a great story teller. I have to thank my father in law too for his stories and his funny jokes. What a blast!

I have to thank all my wonderful cousins and friends. I pick and choose my friends and they are truly exceptional people. They have made me happy and make me look forward to my days and evenings and times spent together. I will always appreciate their kindness and special words they give me. For lifting my spirits when I felt down. I will always give them anything I have to make them happy too. I am also including my kids friends too, because we have become so close that I feel they are my family too.

My sisters are fabulous too. Thank God for my wonderful sisters. My sister Phyllis, who likes to be called Phylly, keeps us amused with all her animals and her funny ways. It was great growing up with her. We were always together and I felt very proud to have her by my side. My sister Lorraine, with her kind and caring ways is great to be with too. We are a close family.

It is very important to stay close to your siblings. No matter how bad things get, don't ever part from your family. Yes, we've had lots and lots of altercations, as other siblings do, but never stay mad and not speak to each other again. This does not show good moral judgment. Be a role model for your kids. By you always staying connected to the family, your kids will always do the same with their brothers and sisters.

Okay...I'm sure there is so much more to talk about, but I will leave it there for now.

Well, have to go. Love you all. Sincerely, Paula

Dirty Delish Dish...........

Here are some delish dishes I've created for you and your family to enjoy. I used to give my recipes to my facebook friends. They all would love it, and they couldn't wait for the next recipe for the day. Please enjoy these easy, fast, healthy and natural recipes From Me TO YOU! Luv ya.

Pasta Alla Puttanesca: This is a recipe made especially for the man in your life. It comes with a variety" of different ingredients....if you know what I mean.
Sauté garlic in olive oil until sizzling. Add gaetta olives, capers, and very small pieces of eggplant. Sauté for a few minutes. Add one can of all natural tomato sauce or fresh tomatoes, cut up. Bring to boil. Then lower heat and simmer for ten minutes. Serve over pasta. Buon Appetito!!

On the menu: Chicken Genovese: Cut up boneless chicken breast into small pieces. Sauté chicken in extra-virgin....guys, stay on track....until golden brown. Add three sliced onions. Stir consistently. When onions are golden, add water just to cover chicken. Bring to a boil, then simmer for 40 minutes. Serve over pasta. You'll luv this dish!!

On the menu: Beef Stew: Cut Sirloin into small pieces. Sauté in olive oil until browned. Add two garlic cloves, one sliced onion, and one beef boullion cube. Stir.Add water to cover meat. Then add carrots and sliced potatoes. Bring to boil and then lower fire and simmer for 40 minutes!! Serve over rice or pasta.

On the menu: Chicken Cacciatore: For the Breast men in your family.... Place breast tenderloins on foil. Sprinkle with salt and pepper. Place in flour. Add to preheated olive oil in frying pan. Sauté until golden. Add cut up poblano or red peppers and garlic. Sauté for two minutes. Add ¼ cup red wine. Let evaporate. Add one can tomato sauce. Bring to boil. Then lower flame, cover and simmer for 45 minutes. Serve over pasta. This dish will surely spice things up tonight!!

On the menu: Chicken Cacciatore without the sauce and for the man who likes it HOT!!!
Salt and pepper chicken like above. Add flour. Sauté in extra virgin— ohhh behave now....olive oil until golden. Add cut up jalopeno peppers, garlic and onion. Sauté for a few minutes. Add ¼ cup white wine- - optional.

Add enough water or chicken broth to cover chicken. Cover, bring to boil, then lower flame and simmer for 45 minutes. This all natural dish will surely light up your palate!

On the menu: Escarole and Bean Soup! Oh no….beans. This wonderful soup will surely cleanse your soul and add rumble too. Clean fresh escarole and set aside. Sauté bacon until cooked. Add three sliced garlic cloves. Keep stirring. Add escarole and stir until softened. Add three cans of cannelloni beans. Add one large can of chicken broth. Salt and pepper to taste. Add two bay leaves. Bring to boil. Then lower flame and simmer for 10 to 15 minutes. Serve with any small soup pasta. Always cook your pasta on the side.

Dirty Delish Dish……… From Me To You!

On the menu: Pasta and Bean Soup. Sauté bacon in olive oil until cooked. Add garlic. Add one can of tomato sauce. Salt and pepper to taste. Add three cans cannelloni beans. Add two large potatoes cut up. Add two bay leaves, one teaspoon dried oregano and crushed hot red pepper to taste. Add one large can of chicken broth plus a cup of water. Bring to boil. Lower heat and simmer for ten minutes. Then scoop out some beans and potatoes and smash with a fork. Add it back to the soup and cook an additional twenty minutes. Serve with small pasta. Buon Appetito!!

On the menu: Chicken Soup. This is the key to a healthy life. There is nothing like a little chicken soup, especially on a cold day to soothe the soul… Place two chicken breast with ribs in a pot with water..enough to cover chicken. Add two inions chopped up. Bring to a boil. Lower heat and add one large can of chicken broth, carrots and celery. Cook for one hour. Serve with pasta. When chicken is cooked, cut it up and add back into the soup. Luv ya

On another note….here are some ideas on what to put together on a dinner menu. The recipes for the meats are to follow.

On the menu: A lovely eye round roast, mashed potatoes, corn, hot, fried jalopeno peppers....to spice things up.... A lovely salad with extra onions...the way my hunny likes it, and crispy Italian bread. Yummy.

Place eye round in a foil lined pan. Preheat oven 450 degrees. Poke holes in roast beef and add cloves of garlic in each slit. Place cut up inions on top of roast. Salt and pepper and drizzle olive oil on top. Place in oven and cook at 450 degrees for 15 minutes. Then lower heat to 375 degrees for the remaining 40 to 45 minutes. Enjoy. This meat is lean and very good for the family. Lots of protein too.

On the menu: Roast pork tenderloin. Place two tenderloins in foil lined pan. Preheat oven 450 degrees. Add these ingredients on top of loins: salt and pepper, garlic, soy sauce, teriyaki sauce, ketchup and olive oil. Add a little water in pan too. Bake for 15 minutes at 450 degrees then lower to 385 degrees for the remaining 45 minutes. You can cover the tenderloins with loose foil towards the end of the baking period to keep from drying up. You'll love this juicy and tender meat as it melts in your mouth. Delish!!!!

On the menu: Veal Stew. This is so simple, you'll make it often. Sauté veal stew in pot in extra virgin olive oil until browned. Add salt and pepper to taste. Add three garlic cloves and simmer. Add two or three sliced potatoes and add water to cover. Bring to boil, then lower and simmer for remaining 20 to 30 minutes. Serve over pasta!

On the menu: Spaghetti with fresh tomatoes. This is my favorite recipe. I can have this every day!!! This is so delicious and simple that you will make this quite often. Cut six ripe, plum tomatoes or vine tomatoes into pieces in bowl. Save all juices in bowl. In a pot, sauté four garlic cloves, sliced until sizzling. Add tomatoes, salt, pepper and fresh basil and cover. Bring to a boil, then lower fire to a simmer and sauté for 15 minutes longer. Keep stirring and smashing tomatoes in pot with a fork until melted. Serve over pasta with crispy Italian bread. Luv ya

You can add fresh basil to sauce while cooking.

On the menu: "Paula's Chicken" A very close friend of mine named this dish for me. She made me laugh too. I always think of her when I make this. Thanks, Tammy!!

Place chicken legs and breasts {with ribs} in a foil lined pan. Preheat oven at 475 degrees. Just a note on ovens...... If you are cooking with a flame oven, you need to lessen the degrees, because the flame ovens tend to give off more heat. If it's an electric oven, you need to cook in a higher temperature than normal.

Okay...back to the chicken. Sprinkle salt and pepper, two onions sliced and drizzle olive oil over chicken. Place in oven and cook for one hour. You'll enjoy this easy, delish dish....I assure you!!

On the menu: Chicken cutlets and ham and cheese or Chicken Cord en blu. Preheat oven at 425 degrees. Place each chicken cutlet in bread crumbs and set aside. Have sliced mozzarella and sliced ham on the side. Foil line a pan. Place one breaded cutlet in pan and place one slice cheese and ham. Cover with another slice of chicken cutlet so as to have two cutlets for one portion. Sprinkle with salt and pepper. Place one slice of butter underneath and on top of each portion. Drizzle a little olive oil on top of each portion too. Bake for one hour and place a foil on top of chicken through the last half hour of cooking. This is so easy and healthy for you all. Enjoy!!

On the menu: Broccoli Soup. Clean and cut broccoli into halves. In a deep pot, sauté sliced onions and garlic in olive oil. Add one or two sliced tomatoes. Salt and pepper to taste. The aroma right now will be so tantalizing..... Add the chopped broccoli and add water or one large can of chicken broth. Add a half a teaspoon of salt. Bring to a boil, and then lower and simmer for twenty more minutes or until broccoli is tender. Serve with noodles or acini pepe...my favorite!!! Any pasta will do.....

Cauliflower Soup: Do the same as the above but just substitute the broccoli with the cauliflower. There....that was easy.

On the menu: Pasta graciatta: Meaning....Dirty Pasta.
Now, remember...when you read one of the main ingredients in this

recipe, you might not want to make it. Don't worry and don't tell the kids the main ingredient. Just serve and they will love it. You'll see.

In a deep pot, fill with water and bring to a boil. Clean and cut cauliflower and place in boiling water. When the cauliflower is tender, take it out with a slotted spoon and set aside. Keep or reserve the water for the pasta later.

In a large skillet or pan, saute sliced garlic and add a tiny can of rolled fillets of anchovies and capers with its liquid. Keep stirring until the fish is melted. Add the softened cauliflower and add water just enough at half way covering the vegetable. Simmer for ten minutes at a very low flame, covered. Serve with pasta.

This dish tends to be on the dry side so it's meant to serve two or four people. If you were to cook for six people, double the recipe.

On the menu: Spaghetti and clams: Clean a dozen or two dozen clams in water. Scrub them clean with a sponge. Set aside in a dish. In a saucepan, sauté lots of garlic until it sizzles. Add the clams to the high flame and cover. Add salt and pepper. When the clams open, add a bottle of clam juice to the mixture. Bring to boil and then lower flame and simmer for 15 minutes. That's it!! Serve over spaghetti.

If you would prefer a red sauce, after the clams open, add a half of can tomato sauce along with the clam juice. Then just do the same as above.

On the menu: King crab claws fra diavolo: In a large, deep pot, saute lots of garlic until it sizzles. Add one can of tomato sauce. Bring to a boil. Add salt and chopped red pepper to the sauce. Add the king crab claws. Cook on high heat for five minutes. Lower flame to a simmer and cook for an additional 15 minutes. Serve over linguini. Make sure you have lots of paper towels, because this dish is sure to get messy when eaten. Your kids will enjoy breaking open the claws. If you have nut crackers, this tends to help. Otherwise…your teeth will do just fine. Just kidding, but that's what I ultimately use.

On the menu: Spaghetti and squid. This is truly a delish dish for the fish lover in you.

Clean squid under running cold water. Cut the tip of the body with a scissor. Stick your finger inside the body and pull out any jelly remains. Don't get squirmish!! After they are cleaned, cut with a scissor to make little circles. Set aside in a bowl.

In a saucepan, sauté garlic and add your squid and keep stirring for a few seconds. Add your sauce, cover and bring to a boil. Lower heat and simmer covered for 15, 20 minutes. Serve over spaghetti. Remember to always add your salt and pepper to taste.

On the menu: Lentil Soup. This is a very hearty, delicious soup. Full of protein too.

Soak a bag of dried lentils for one hour or more in cold water. When softened, rinse and set aside. In a large pot, sauté bacon until cooked. Add sliced onions, garlic and cut up carrots. Add the lentils and stir. Add one large can of Chicken broth or water. You can always add more water as you cook if you prefer it more soupy. Add two bay leaves, salt and pepper. Cover. Bring to a boil, then lower flame and simmer covered for one and a half hours. Always check the pot to see if you have to add more water, because sometimes it gets dried out quicker than expected. Serve with pasta – optional.

On the menu: This is one of my specialties that is loved by everyone, esp. Judith.

Sauce with Pork. At the butcher, ask for pork ribs with bones. It's something like a sparerib.

In a large, deep pot, sauté the pork in extra virgin olive oil until browned. This is tricky. You have to stand there and keep turning the meat to brown all sides. If you are not an experienced cook, please wear an oven mitt and use a long fork.

When the meat is browned, add one or two sliced onions. This is the key. When the onions are softened, add one can of sauce. Cover, bring to a boil. Then simmer covered for one hour. I assure you… this will be your favorite recipe yet!! Serve over pasta and enjoy the juicy, tender meat falling off the bone and into your mouth. Mmmmmm…..almost as good as……..ooops….that's another book!! Luv ya

On the menu: Fried Peppers. This can be any type of fresh pepper:

Jalopeno, Poblano, Long hot Peppers, Sweet Peppers, etc. Make sure peppers are dry and not wet.

For the non experienced chef….be careful. You have to stay by this dish as you are preparing from the start to the finish. You can not leave your pot at all!! I suggest you wear an oven mitt and use a long fork to turn your peppers. Have the lid ready to cover if the peppers begin to splash.

In a frying pan, heat extra virgin olive oil – about a quarter cup- until hot or a few seconds. Add the cut up peppers gently into the hot oil. Let stay for two minutes on one side and then flip to the other. You will see them have a brownish, or blackish tint in some areas. This is when it's ready to flip. Then take out and reserve the oil for dipping with your crispy Italian bread. You will love this.

If you would like the idea of fried peppers but you don't like the risk or the mess, you can bake the peppers in the oven.

If you have any questions, you can contact me on Facebook for a more detailed version of my recipes.

Luv you and remember….these are all homemade dishes to bring your family and husband up in. They will give you a kiss after every meal.

On the menu: Best Beef Braciole

This can be substituted with Pork braciole. Pork tends to be much more tender and tastier. If you prefer the beef, make sure you bang out your meat. This is called tenderizing.

Lay meat flat. Place grated Romano cheese, dried or fresh parsley and hard boiled egg slices in center. Salt and pepper to taste. Roll and secure tightly with toothepics. Make sure to tell your guest about the toothe picks and place always three every time.

Place extra virgin olive oil in pot. Place rolls of braciole into pot and simmer until browned. Keep turning them. After they are browned, add one sliced onion and simmer a little. Add one can of sauce. Add salt and pepper. Bring to a boil. Lower fire and simmer for 45 minutes. Serve over pasta. This will be a hit at the dinner table. Buon appetito with love!!!

Why Mermaids?! As you can see, I have included some of my artwork in this book. I chose to include mermaids because this is my fantasy line. Mermaids are a symbol of everlasting life, beauty, strength, courage, sensuality and goodness. Since one of my theories explain discovering the "Fountain of Youth," I thought it would be fun to include these images to you. My fantasy line is just one of my many mediums of art that I create. These paintings are done on glass with an old Italian reverse painting. It is very difficult and most impressive when seen in its true color and depth. Even though my life was devoted to my children and husband, I have always found peace in creating my art, and I thank my family for putting up with all my ventures, the ups and downs of my inventions. I thank them for all their compliments, and I also thank my mother and Aunt Lydia for always giving me the encouragement to never give up in my artwork or endeavors Their patience is greatly appreciated and kept my soul alive. With all my love, Paula Sole